SISTERS
A Modern Girl's Guide
to Serving a Mission

SISTERS

A Modern Girl's Guide
to Serving a Mission

MELISSA DYMOCK

Covenant Communications, Inc.

Cover image *Book Club* © 2013 BriAnna Shultz, iStockphotography.com

Cover design copyright © 2013 by Covenant Communications, Inc.

Published by Covenant Communications, Inc.
American Fork, Utah

Printed in the United States of America
First Printing: March 2012

19 18 17 16 15 14 13   10 9 8 7 6 5 4 3 2

ISBN: 978-1-60861-969-6

TABLE OF CONTENTS

INTRODUCTION

Six months before my twenty-first birthday, I was faced with the most difficult decision of my life. Should I go on a mission? That decision and the ensuing months of preparation had me asking a lot of questions. The first was, of course, whether I should really go. Young men are expected to, but everyone has different opinions about young women going. Some feel that missionary work is the responsibility of the priesthood, others think sisters should go, and others believe a girl should just focus on marriage. The decision can be difficult.

Once I decided to go, I was faced with other questions: How do I prepare? What do I buy? What if I don't like my companion? What about school? Do I know enough about the gospel? Like many other young women, as I looked for answers, I had a difficult time finding talks or advice specifically for sister missionaries.

I searched the *Ensign* and similar materials, and the only talk I found with advice for a sister preparing to serve was from the 1970s titled, "A Letter to Girls about Lady Missionaries."[1] Some of its advice included, "Sleep

---

1. Lana Mangelson, "A Letter to Girls about Lady Missionaries," *Ensign,* Oct. 1972, 20.

on a satin pillowcase; this preserves hair style and also femininity." It also admonished sisters to hold a periodic "Be Nice to Elders Week," where they would make food for the elders. This wasn't the kind of advice I was in need of nor apt to follow.

I didn't know any returned sister missionaries well enough to ask my many questions, so the next eighteen months were a leap of faith in every sense of the word. While on my mission, my companions and I would talk about what we wished we'd known before and what we would tell other sisters who were considering and preparing for missions. When I arrived home and met these sisters, I answered their several questions, but I kept thinking that they needed a resource.

This book's purpose is not to push you to go. But if you've ever considered serving a mission or are about to go, I invite you to browse these pages; my prayer is that something here will help you get a little closer to your goal. You might begin reading this book and decide that a traditional mission isn't for you. That's fine, but don't stop reading. The lessons in this book are life lessons, applicable in settings outside a mission. They just happen to be lessons learned by those serving missions as well.

I have interviewed companions, leaders, co-workers, friends, and friends of friends to help you in answering whatever questions you may have with regard to a mission. These sisters (and brethren) can help us understand the wide array of choices available to young women. Most of the sisters I interviewed served a mission; however, some married instead or focused on schooling or work. Others merely postponed their mission until the time was right. Whatever their decisions were, they all had one thing in common: They asked the Lord what He wanted of them and then faithfully followed His counsel.

CHAPTER 1
Should You Serve a Mission?

Does the Lord need or want you to serve a mission?

IN 1977, SPENCER W. KIMBALL ANNOUNCED, "'Every worthy young man should fill a mission.' The Lord expects him to fill a mission."[2] Every time I heard that quote, I couldn't help wondering, *But what about me? What do the prophets say about me, a young woman?* While young men may question whether or not they will go on missions, they never have to ask if they should.

When a sister turns nineteen, she has the opportunity to serve a mission, but should she? She deals with questions young men never have to: Does the Lord *want* me to serve a mission? Does the Church even need me to serve a mission? Will I miss out on an opportunity for marriage if I go? These questions are tricky because there isn't an all-encompassing yes or no answer. The decision ultimately lies with each individual sister and requires a great deal of prayer and pondering.

Because not as much is said about sister missionaries as about the elders, sisters often feel confused as to what is expected of them in regard to a mission. The advice of the First Presidency concerning sister missionaries is that "Sisters can make a valuable contribution . . . but they

2. Spencer W. Kimball, "It Becometh Every Man," *Liahona,* Nov. 1977, 1.

should not be pressured to serve. Bishops should not recommend them for missionary service if it will interfere with imminent marriage prospects."[3] Confirming the First Presidency's message, Elder Ballard said, "A full-time mission is totally appropriate for a young woman, if that is what she wants to do and she is worthy. If they have prospects for marriage, that is a higher calling."[4]

The fact that the choice to serve a mission is solely up to the individual sister can make her feel alone in her decision. This, of course, isn't entirely true—all of us have been given the gift of the Holy Ghost—but this may be the first big decision in a young woman's life where she has to rely on it so completely.

So how do you decide? It takes a great deal of prayer and study. It takes faith to listen for the right answer and courage to put your life in the Lord's hands. There is no one answer for every sister. And, unfortunately, it's rare for the heavens to part and for God to say, "Go on a mission!" in a large, booming, unmistakable voice.

How do you decide if you should go on a mission?

President James E. Faust taught that the "still, small voice . . . speaks to all of us through the scriptures, modern prophets, and personal revelation."[5] In the Doctrine and Covenants, the Lord states, "I will tell you in your mind and in your heart" (8:2).

---

3. Richard G. Scott, "Now Is the Time to Serve a Mission," *Ensign,* May 2006, 88.
4. M. Russell Ballard, "How to Prepare to Be a Good Missionary," *Liahona,* Mar. 2007, 10–15.
5. James E. Faust, "Did You Get the Right Message?" *Ensign,* May 2004, 62.

What you have to learn is how the Spirit speaks to *you*. Some people are more in tune with the Spirit—they are gifted in that regard—but others have to struggle for an answer. No matter which way you learn, you are entitled to an answer. The Lord promises that.

For some sisters, the Spirit speaks through emotion— the decision to serve a mission *feels* right. For others, the answer is a thought that comes with complete clarity, one they know didn't come from them. Ellie[6] had such an answer. She had no intention of serving a mission and, quite honestly, no desire. That's why she knew the strong impression that said, "You need to go on a mission," didn't come from her. She hadn't been praying about it or even thinking about it. Perhaps the Lord knew that a clear command was the only way He would get through to her.

Other sisters plan on serving a mission their whole lives, and when the time to serve comes, they have no misgivings about going. It isn't so much that they feel they should go but that going is fine with the Lord.

For other sisters, the idea of going on a mission comes slowly. They start thinking about it but are unsure it's the path they should take. So they begin to pray about it and ask for guidance. Eventually, they start to feel more inclined toward one decision.

Often the Lord requires more than just asking. In a revelation given to Joseph Smith on behalf of Oliver Cowdery, the Lord told Oliver how he could recognize the Spirit in making a decision. He said,

> Behold, you have not understood; you
> have supposed that I would give it unto

6. Name has been changed.

you, when you took no thought save it was to ask me.

But, behold, I say unto you, that you must study it out in your mind; then you must ask me if it be right, and if it is right I will cause that your bosom shall burn within you; therefore, you shall feel that it is right.

But if it be not right you shall have no such feelings, but you shall have a stupor of thought that shall cause you to forget the thing which is wrong." (D&C 9:7–9)

The Lord teaches that you must study the decision in your mind and then ask Him about it. In following this process, remember that you may not necessarily forget the other alternatives. You will simply not be at peace with those choices. Or you may hit a roadblock as you mentally pursue a certain course, experiencing a "stupor of thought."

Liz had always planned to serve a mission. However, when she turned twenty-one, she found herself in a relationship. Still, she was determined to serve a mission. She went so far as to receive her call, but she didn't feel sure of her decision anymore. In fact, she felt great trepidation. She thought that in receiving her call, she would feel peace, but she never received the confirmation she had anticipated. After a great deal of prayer and deciding not to go, she felt a calmness return to her. Her stupor of thought was gone.

A mission is a big decision. Before praying, you need to think about what this will mean for you—for your career, for your relationships, and for your family.

Can you put these things on hold without becoming resentful? Can you walk away from your boyfriend, possibly forever, and trust in the Lord? When a few men offered to follow Christ (after they took care of a few things), Jesus told them, "No man, having put his hand to the plough, and looking back, is fit for the kingdom of God" (Luke 9:62). Are you able to put your hand to the plow and not look back?

In studying it out, consider the reasons you want to serve a mission. Is it because it's expected of you, or is it because you truly want to serve the Lord? Talk to other women who have served missions; they can help you know what to expect. Talk to your family and leaders; they can't make the decision for you, but they can offer a different perspective than your own. And at the end of all this, talk to the Lord. Tell Him what you feel, what you want, and then let Him know that you'll follow the promptings He gives you.

Why should you have to go through all this when the Lord could simply tell you what to do? The Lord expects us to use our agency and wants us to learn to recognize the Spirit. We may only need a confirmation and may come to the right decision before we even go to the Lord. Remember what the Lord says about taking the initiative: "For behold, it is not meet that I should command in all things; for he that is compelled in all things, the same is a slothful and not a wise servant" (D&C 58:26). It's also possible that all this preparation gives you time to accept the Lord's will so that when the answer does come, you're ready for it. A mission isn't for everyone, and it doesn't mean you are any less spiritual if you aren't meant to go. In fact, it takes as much spiritual maturity to follow the Spirit when the answer is no as when it's yes.

Some of you may be saying, "But I've done everything you've suggested, and I can't get an answer!" There are reasons why you might not have received or recognized an answer:

> 1. You may have received an answer but not in the way you expected or wanted—it wasn't accompanied by thunder, lightning, or a burning bush. Take a step back. Did you receive an answer in a small, simple way but chose to disregard it? Did you receive an answer but keep asking in the hope that the Lord will change His mind? The prophet Jonah tried to escape the Lord's call to preach in Nineveh by taking a ship to another country. While en route, his ship was about to be destroyed in a storm, and the sailors, knowing he was the reason the Lord was destroying the ship, tossed Jonah into the ocean, where he was swallowed by a whale. After repenting, Jonah was freed from the whale and went on his mission to Nineveh.[7] Hopefully it doesn't take being swallowed by a whale for you to accept the Lord's answer.

> 2. Are you in a position where you can readily feel the Spirit of the Lord? President Faust teaches us that "we have to work at being tuned in [to the Spirit]. Most of us

---

7. Jonah 1–3.

need a long time to become tuned in."[8] We must train ourselves through living the standards of the Church and by heeding the still, small voice. With the Spirit, as with a cell phone, there are some places you can't get service. Look at your life and remove the sins that are blocking clear reception. And don't be afraid of silence. Turn everything off—yes, even your cell phone—and see if you can't hear or feel something. Sometimes the Spirit can't be heard through all the noise in our lives.

3. When the Lord gives you an answer, He will hold you accountable for it. Perhaps He knows you're not ready to follow His decision and doesn't want to bring you under condemnation. When you're ready to follow His counsel, whatever that may be, you'll receive it. President Eyring said, "To know His will you must be committed to do it. The words 'Thy will be done,' written in the heart, are the window to revelation."[9]

4. Now may not be the right time. Sarah kept asking for an answer but did not receive one for a long time After a while, she put the idea aside and moved on with life. A year or so later, she began thinking about it again and received her answer. If

---

8. James E. Faust, "Did You Get the Right Message?" *Ensign,* May 2004, 67.

9. Henry B. Eyring, "Rise to Your Call," *Liahona,* Nov. 2002, 76.

the Lord says you should go on a mission, you may have to exercise patience and wait for the timing to be right. If He says not to go on a mission, you might miss the "at least not right now" message and determine to never serve a mission. Live your life so you're in tune enough with the Spirit that you can trust in the Lord's timing.

Remember, you're not choosing between good or evil, so you may not receive a strong answer either way. At this point in their lives, many sisters are furthering their education, considering marriage, or making other plans for the future. Any of these courses may be acceptable to the Lord. The decision to serve a mission may be completely yours. The Lord may want to see what decision you will make without being commanded or compelled. Would you willingly give your life for the next eighteen months, even if the Lord didn't request it?

Sometimes you just need to make a decision and move forward. If it feels wrong, change your decision. Sometimes you don't know which is the right path until you take one. And once you've made a decision, stay open to what the Lord has to tell you. Even if you may not feel it's right or wrong, make a decision. Often the right path becomes clear to you awhile later. I decided more than six months before my twenty-first birthday that I was going on a mission, but I waited a few months before I told anyone, just in case things changed.

Two roommates decided to serve missions at the same time and began filling out their papers together. One served a traditional eighteen-month mission, and the other promptly met her future husband, so she decided to remain home. They both received calls, just to different places and assignments. Some sisters feel good about serving a mission, but then another path presents itself and they end up not going. When this happens, some wonder if they misunderstood the prompting to begin preparing. But wise sisters soon realize that preparing for a mission prepares a person for life. Remember, sometimes the only purpose in going down one road is that it leads you to another.

Whatever you decide, be willing to do what the Lord wants you to do in whatever capacity you are called.

Is a mission for you?

One of the biggest hurdles I faced in deciding to go on a mission was my fear of becoming the stereotypical sister missionary. You know the woman I mean: a homely know-it-all who either thinks she's better than all the elders or a homely know-nothing who spends her mission baking for the elders. I didn't want to be labeled as one of these sisters, and I didn't want to serve with one. As a child, I was told that the only women who went on missions were the women who had nothing better to do or who couldn't find husbands and thought the mission field provided an ideal ratio of men to women. I just didn't want the stigmas attached.

I was just completing my junior year in college, was excited about my career prospects, and felt I was too young to be married. Since I didn't fit the mold, I seriously wondered if the mission field was the right place for me. I had never considered a mission as part of my future. I was on a tight four-year plan to finish school and begin my career.

Six months before my twenty-first birthday, I was sitting in Sunday school waiting for class to start when the thought that I needed to go on a mission popped into my head. I looked around to see who the Spirit was talking to and was shocked to realize it was me. After church, I told my roommate that I was considering going on a mission, and she said, "You're kidding." I told her that's what I'd said to the Spirit. Keep in mind, this wasn't an issue of worthiness; it's just that I had never considered a mission.

I immediately decided I wouldn't rush the decision but would give it prayerful consideration. I vacillated back and forth over the next two weeks. I felt the Lord was pleased with my choice to attend college and wouldn't punish me if I stayed. After the initial prompting to serve a mission, I didn't receive any more revelation. It was as if Heavenly Father was saying, "This is what I think, but the choice is ultimately yours. I will support you no matter your choice." I felt He was waiting to see what I was willing to lay on the altar.

I talked with people whose opinions I trusted, and the answer I kept receiving was that if I did go, I would never regret it. I think deep down I knew what my decision would be; I just had to come to terms with it. I called my brother one night and blurted out, "I'm thinking about going on a mission. What do you think?"

"What do you want to do?"

"I want to go."

"So go," he said.

When I entered the Missionary Training Center, I thought I was in the minority in regard to why I had decided to serve a mission. I believed that most sisters had always planned on serving or didn't have anything better to do. I was wrong.

I soon learned that most sisters were like myself; they were as surprised by the call as I was. Many sisters had boyfriends who were either waiting for them at home or on missions themselves. Some had broken off engagements because it hadn't felt right and then found themselves with mission papers in their hands. Many had a college degree or were well on their way to one. Some had walked away from incredible career opportunities.

One sister had no intention of serving a mission despite the constant encouragement of her parents. Then one day, she attended the temple and didn't feel the Spirit with her. She said a little prayer to bring her thoughts in line. When the question "Should I go on a mission?" jumped from her lips, it surprised her. The yes that followed came so strongly that she couldn't deny it.

Some sisters left their countries and families. One Mongolian sister was disowned by her mother when she accepted a call to serve in the United States. A few sisters had planned on missions since childhood, but they were the minority. Some did go for husbands, but, luckily, they were few and far between. A mission is for any worthy sister who wants to serve the Lord.

Are you worthy to serve a mission?

Many sisters worry that they aren't worthy enough to serve a mission. They look at their sins and weaknesses and feel they will never be called. Know that there has never been a perfect sister called on a mission. All sister missionaries have had sins to repent of and weaknesses to overcome. Only through the Atonement can anyone be worthy to serve.

Remember the Fourth Article of Faith: "We believe that the first principles and ordinances of the Gospel are:

first, Faith in the Lord Jesus Christ; second, Repentance; third, Baptism by immersion for the remission of sins; fourth, Laying on of hands for the gift of the Holy Ghost." Not only do missionaries teach these principles for eighteen months; these are the principles they must live by. By adhering to these simple principles, you can be worthy to serve a mission.

It begins with faith. With faith in Christ, you believe His teachings and strive to become like Him. During this process, you recognize many of your failings, and so you begin to feel guilt. Use this guilt to bring you to repentance—that is its purpose.

Once you have repented, you are ready to receive forgiveness and partake in the Atonement by being born again in the waters of baptism. But wait, you say, what if I have already been baptized? This is where the sacrament comes in. Each week, when we take the sacrament, we are renewing our baptismal covenants, and if we clearly understand what the sacrament does for us, we know we may become as clean as we were at baptism. Only through this process can we be worthy to have the Holy Ghost with us. During the sacramental prayers, the priests bless the bread and water that the partakers might "*always* have his Spirit to be with them" (Moroni 4:3; 5:2; emphasis added). This process is cyclic and continual. It is not something you do every few years or just when you've sinned big. It's for every day. And it is only through Christ and this process that you can be worthy to bear His name in the mission field.

Some are burdened by the memory of a terrible sin, one they may have properly repented of but which they continue to dwell on. Alma the Younger spoke of repentance to his son Corianton, who had sinned his way out of the mission field by becoming involved with a woman. Alma taught him about justice and repentance then told him, "My son, I desire that ye should let these things trouble you no more, and only let your sins trouble you, with that trouble which shall bring you down unto repentance" (Alma 42:29). The purpose of guilt is to bring you to repentance. Once you have repented, let go of the guilt. The guilt that brings you to repentance is of God; the guilt that makes you feel unable to be loved by God is of Satan. Be careful to recognize the difference. The Spirit will help you know when you are on the right track.

John, after years of inactivity, returned to the Church and eventually was standing before the stake president for a temple recommend. He was asked if he had a testimony of the Atonement. John replied yes. Then the stake president asked if he was worthy to go to the temple and, burdened by the memory of his many sins, John said no. The stake president asked him again if he had a testimony of the Atonement, and the man replied that he did. The stake president again asked, "Are you worthy to go to the temple?" and John said no. He wept and replied that he wasn't even worthy to pray to Heavenly Father; he could only approach Him in the name of Jesus Christ. So once more, the stake president asked him if he had a testimony of the Atonement. Then the stake president explained that, as with prayer, only through Christ could the man be worthy to enter the temple. If he truly believed in the power of the Atonement and applied it, then he could be worthy to enter the temple. For the first time, the man understood that because of the Atonement, he could be worthy to be in the presence of the Father.

The question of worthiness to serve a mission is a personal one. You will be interviewed by both your bishop and your stake president. Be honest with them. If there is a sin you are still battling, tell them. It isn't a weight you want to be carrying around anymore. Know that through the Atonement, the Savior can lift your burdens and make you worthy to stand in the presence of the Father. And if, for whatever reason, you are not extended a call to serve a traditional mission, remember there are numerous ways to serve the Lord. Don't let this be a deterrent to living a life dedicated to the gospel.

Are you qualified to serve a mission?

Many prospective sister missionaries wonder if they are qualified to serve a mission. They worry that their testimony isn't strong enough or that they don't know enough about the doctrines of the gospel.

In a revelation concerning missionaries given to Joseph Smith in 1829, the Lord said, "Therefore, if ye have desires to serve God ye are called to the work" (D&C 4:3). One of the most important qualifications in serving a mission is a desire to serve God. If you want to serve a mission for any other reason besides wanting to serve the Lord, you probably need to rethink the decision because desire to do the Lord's will is the driving force behind missionary work. Desire is what gets you there, keeps you going, and carries you to the end.

When your only desire is to serve the Lord, He will be able to use you as an instrument in His hands and will qualify you for the work, *choosing* you to carry out His purposes. Remember, "There are many called, but few are chosen" (D&C 121:34). A missionary may be "called" to serve a mission, but is she chosen? Doctrine and Covenants, section 4—which, by the way, you will be memorizing at the MTC—teaches us how we are chosen for the work: by striving to attain vital qualities such as faith, hope, charity, and love, with an eye single to the glory of God. You may not have all of these qualities before you enter the field, but these are the characteristics you need to focus on developing.

As the first principle of the gospel, faith is the foundation on which you build your testimony. Every month, members stand at the podium and speak with conviction about their knowledge of gospel principles, but all knowledge begins with faith. Some prospective missionaries may question their testimony because they don't know all they think they should. Some are concerned that they don't *know* the Church is true. But Alma the Younger teaches us that "faith is not to have a perfect knowledge of things" (Alma 32:21). He defines faith as a "hope for things which are not seen, which are true" (Alma 32:21).

Can you serve a mission even if your faith hasn't progressed to knowledge? As Alma suggests, you don't have to know everything there is to know. Faith is where you begin. A person's faith may progress to knowledge in certain principles of the gospel but still be lacking in other areas. Alma teaches us that faith begins with desire, and he compares the word to a seed: "Now, if ye give place, that a seed may be planted in your heart, behold, if it be a true seed, or a good seed, if you do not cast it out by your unbelief . . . behold, it will begin to swell within your breasts . . . it beginneth to enlighten [your] understanding" (Alma 32:28).

This swelling increases faith, but Alma warns that your faith still hasn't grown to a perfect knowledge. And yet, as it increases, eventually "your knowledge is perfect in that thing, and your faith is dormant" (Alma 32:34). This happens with principles such as tithing, fasting, and the Word of Wisdom. After faithfully paying tithing and receiving the promised blessings, a person's faith can become perfect in that principle, but they may still struggle with other principles, such as fasting. Notice that an important part of gaining a perfect knowledge of things is in doing something about it. You must *plant* the seed and *nourish* it.

If you wonder if you have a testimony of the gospel or of any gospel principle, you can apply Alma's counsel and ask, "Does it feel right and good? Does it enlighten my understanding?" This is the way you can tell that the Church is true. As you do this, your faith will increase and the Lord will be able to use your testimony to strengthen others' testimonies. So while it is important that a prospective missionary have a strong testimony of the gospel, do not discount yourself from missionary work because your testimony isn't perfect, since no one's is.

The second qualification for missionaries is hope. Why hope? Mormon said, "If a man have faith he must needs have hope; for without faith there cannot be any hope" (Moroni 7:42). The two are inseparably intertwined. Faith is just a stronger manifestation of hope. You hope going on a mission is the right thing. You hope you will reach someone, and you hope your going will make a difference. Without hope, who would ever turn in their papers or set foot on a plane?

The third qualification is charity. In a letter to the Corinthians, the Apostle Paul says, "Though I have the gift of prophecy, and understand all mysteries, and all knowledge; and though I have all faith, so that I could remove mountains, and have not charity, I am nothing" (1 Corinthians 13:2).

Paul's definition of charity describes what a missionary ought to be. A missionary "suffereth long, and is kind; [a missionary] envieth not; . . . Doth not behave [herself] unseemingly, seeketh not her own, is not easily provoked, thinketh no evil; Rejoiceth not in iniquity, but rejoiceth in the truth; Beareth all things, believeth all things, hopeth all things, endureth all things. [A missionary] never faileth" (1 Corinthians 13:4–8).

Do not expect to have all of these qualities before you enter the field. Just know that these are the behaviors you need to focus on developing. Moroni teaches us that "charity is the pure love of Christ" (Moroni 7:47), which takes us to the fourth requirement: love. Missionary service requires a love of God and a love of the gospel. A missionary must love her companion, the work, and the people she serves. In the mission field, however, acquiring and maintaining this love can be difficult. How do you love someone who yells at you and slams the door in your face? Some companions are your best friends; some you might compare to your worst enemy. It can be difficult to love being a missionary, especially on days when the work is almost nonexistent. Those days might tempt you to shake a fist at the heavens. The only thing to do is to serve those around you and pray your patience outlasts your frustration. These are the times when praying for charity with all the energy of heart is the only course of action.

And lastly, a missionary must have an "eye single to the glory of God" (D&C 4:5). This is when we put our hand to the plow without looking back, making sure that our course is straight and on track. When you enter the MTC, thoughts of home don't magically disappear. But you don't dwell upon what you've left behind, and that includes family, friends, boyfriends, school, and careers. You have to work at focusing on mission work.

It took one sister nine months in the field to accomplish this. Sarah knew she had accomplished it when, while riding her bike, she realized that had she stayed home, this would have been the day she would have graduated from college. She felt no regret, only relief that she had made the right decision.

So, should *you* go on a mission? Ask the Lord and then go to work to develop the characteristics that will qualify you for service in the field and in life.

CHAPTER 2
The Papers and the Call

Filling out your papers

So you've decided to go. If you're at least nineteen or soon will be, it's time to start your application. In an article in the *New Era,* David A. Edwards recommends starting the process at least four months before you are available to serve a mission.[10] The sooner you get your papers turned in, the sooner you can receive your call.

Make an appointment with your bishop for a personal interview and talk with him about your decision if you haven't already. He will provide you with the information you need to start filling out your paperwork online. In most cases, you won't get actual papers but will apply at LDS.org after your bishop provides you with a username and password. If you don't have online access, he will give you the actual papers. You will still print off the medical portion to have your doctors fill out, and then you will return those to your bishop.

Immediately make appointments with your doctor and dentist for a physical and dental checkup. Many sisters wonder why this step is required. It's simple—a mission is physically and mentally demanding. If you have any underlying physiological or psychological issues, a mission

10. See David A. Edwards, "Your Call to Serve," *New Era,* March 2007, 15.

will bring them to the forefront. One elder entered the MTC unaware that he suffered from depression. With the shock of a new setting and increased pressures, he dropped forty pounds in a matter of weeks. He was forced to go home. Even perfectly healthy missionaries struggle. In my mission, we used to lie in bed at night comparing our aching legs. Also, depending on where you serve, you might not have access to medical care, so any preexisting medical condition may affect where you're called.

Another reason to schedule medical appointments as soon as possible is that you may need to have work done before you can leave. If you haven't had your wisdom teeth pulled, you'll likely need to. Immunizations such as hepatitis must be given over the course of a few months for full effect.

During this time, you might also want to start the process of applying for a passport. This can take a few months, and you don't want your arrival in the mission field delayed because you're waiting for a passport or a visa.

Once you've finished filling out everything, you will meet with your bishop for a final interview and he will click a button online that submits your application to the stake president. You will then meet with your stake president, who will click the final button online to send everything off to the missionary department.

After your papers are submitted, expect to wait about two to three weeks for your call to arrive in the mail. This can vary, but if you have any concerns, your bishop can check the status online.

Going where the Lord wants you to go

Can you believe you will be living in a place you've never been, possibly speaking a language you've never spoken, for eighteen months? Decide right now that wherever you go, it's where you're supposed to be.

Remember, when you turn in your papers, you are agreeing to go wherever the Lord wants you to go. However remote or humble your place in the vineyard is, you've been called of God. President Eyring said, "The Lord knows you. He knows whom He would have serve in every position in His Church. He chose you. He has prepared a way so that He could issue your call. . . . Your call is an example of a source of power unique to the Lord's Church. Men and women are called of God by prophecy and by the laying on of hands by those God has authorized."[11]

When I decided to go on a mission, I met people who told me they just knew where they were going to go before they received their call. So I picked a place and decided that's where I knew I was going to go. Big mistake. When I opened my call and it didn't say New York, New York, but some unheard-of place—Lubbock, Texas—I half wondered if there had been a mistake.

One elder was sure his call was to the Philippines. The one place he didn't want to go was Germany—it was where his brother went. When he saw his call sitting on the kitchen table, he picked it up and, without even opening it, knew the call was for Germany. He threw the envelope down in disgust and refused to open it for several hours. He was right; it was for Germany.

One of my companions received a phone call while she was at work telling her that her call had come. Her boss asked her where the one place was she didn't want to go. She gave the standard missionary answer: "I'll go

---

11. Henry B. Eyring, "Rise to Your Call," *Liahona*, Nov. 2002, 76.

anywhere the Lord sends me." Her boss refused to accept that answer and asked again. She replied honestly, "West Texas; it's the ugliest place on earth." (Sorry, West Texas. We did change our minds about the area.) Her boss replied, "You realize, your call just changed in the mail."

Learn from those who've gone before. Don't ever pick a place you absolutely don't want to go, and don't second-guess the Lord. If you question your call, you may begin to question your mission.

Being set apart

Just before entering the MTC, you will be set apart as a missionary by your stake president; then he'll give you a blessing. From this moment on, you are a missionary until you're released. "The stake president will remind you of the importance of such service and instruct you concerning how you should live and conduct your affairs. In all probability, he will include in his blessing such promises as the development of a Christlike character, a forgiveness of sins, and the acquisition of unspeakable joy. Nonetheless, these and other stated blessings do not come by the wave of a wand or the sound of the lips. They come in accord with desire and a worthy performance of duty."[12]

When you are set apart for missionary service, you are given the authority to represent Jesus Christ and to preach His gospel. What an incredible responsibility! You may be the only contact some people have with the Church. They will base much of what they think about the Church on what you say and do. Through your diligence in living the gospel and in striving to follow

12. Carlos E. Asay, "Write Your Own Blessing," *New Era*, Oct. 1981, 4.

and honor the Savior, His image will be reflected in your countenance.

Take a minute to think of the words "set apart." Just what exactly are you being set apart from? According to President Spencer W. Kimball, "The setting apart may be taken literally; it is a setting apart from sin, apart from the carnal; apart from everything which is crude, low, vicious, cheap, or vulgar; *set apart* from the world to a higher plane of thought and activity. The blessing is conditional upon faithful performance."[13]

At the MTC, you'll be given a license to preach, a card you will carry with you throughout your mission. This is the Church authorizing you to represent it. I was struck by the words on my card: "Melissa Dymock has been called as worthy to preach the gospel. We invite all to heed her message." When we take these words to heart, we realize that we are in a unique position to bring others to Christ and that our message should be one and the same with that of the Savior.

---

13. *The Teachings of Spencer W. Kimball,* ed. Edward L. Kimball (Salt Lake City: Deseret Book) 1982, 478.

CHAPTER 3
Preparing to Serve

Spiritual Preparation
Testimony

As they go about purchasing various items to sustain them for eighteen months, some missionaries have the tendency to forget the most important item to prepare—their testimony. They procrastinate spiritual preparation, reasoning that there will be plenty of time for studying at the MTC and in the field. Some are under the assumption that the MTC is such a spiritual place that Satan has no influence, but they are wrong. Placing yourself in a spiritual environment does not necessarily make you a spiritual person.

One sister said her attitude just before her mission was that of procrastination. It was all right if she neglected her scriptures because in a few months she would be studying nonstop. She was devastated when she discovered that, upon entering the MTC, her testimony had slipped almost to nothing. Finding that it was much harder for her to regain it, she spent her first week on her knees pleading with God that she would.

When a sister leaves for a mission, she's much like a ship leaving the harbor for the first time. Once the ship sails into open waters, it's vulnerable to the storms of the ocean.

Whatever underlying weaknesses or cracks the ship has will immediately become apparent as leaks, and the ship stands in danger of sinking. It takes precious time to fix these leaks, some of which can't be fixed at sea. It's important that we not waste our precious time at the MTC fixing "leaks"— prepare while you're still in the harbor.

The temple

When many young women think about going to the temple one day, they focus on being sealed to their future husbands and not on the endowment. One blessing about going on a mission is that you're given the opportunity to develop an individual relationship with the Lord through the endowment.

Before entering the MTC, you will receive your own endowment. It is during the initiatory part of this that you receive and begin wearing the temple garments. The initiatory contains more of the promised blessings, while the actual endowment is when you make covenants to God. These covenants will be similar to the ones you made at baptism.

Brigham Young taught, "Your endowment is, to receive all those ordinances in the House of the Lord, which are necessary for you, after you have departed this life, to enable you to walk back to the presence of the Father, . . . and gain your eternal exaltation."[14]

Your ward or stake should offer a temple preparation class. Attend this regularly and study the scriptures, particularly the *Pearl of Great Price*, to better understand the teachings you will receive. Preparing your life for a mission is the same preparation you should use for the temple.

14. In *Journal of Discourses,* 2:31.

Much of the teaching in the temple is done through symbols, so you may not understand or fully appreciate the temple on your first visit. Elder David B. Haight advised temple goers on what to do after your initial visit: "If you may have been somewhat confused, unclear, or concerned about your temple experience, I hope you will return again and again. When you return, come with an open, seeking, contrite heart, and allow the Spirit to teach you by revelation what the symbols can mean to you and the eternal realities which they represent."[15]

Understanding of and appreciation for the temple must come through revelation. Use what you have learned about receiving revelation while you contemplate these new teachings. Understanding also comes through repetition. Visit the temple as often as you are able. I was unable to go through the temple until about a week before I entered the MTC, so I felt ill equipped to teach people about the temple. Don't count on attending the temple often on your mission since there might not even be a temple in your mission.

The temple isn't just about receiving your endowment or those for the dead. Elder Haight further teaches us, "You may freely partake of the promised personal revelation that may bless your life with power, knowledge, light, beauty, and truth from on high, which will guide you and your posterity to eternal life."

Prayer

One way you can prepare spiritually today is to make prayer an active part of your life. The Bible Dictionary

---

15. David B. Haight, "Come to the House of the Lord," *Ensign,* May 1992, 15.

defines prayer as "the act by which the will of the Father and the will of the child are brought into correspondence with each other." It's imperative to your success as a missionary and as a daughter of God that your will be in line with the Father's.

Scripture study

Scripture study is also vital to spiritual survival and missionary preparation. The Lord has said, "Seek not to declare my word, but first seek to obtain my word, and then shall your tongue be loosed; then, if you desire, you shall have my Spirit and my word, yea, the power of God unto the convincing of men" (D&C 11:21). It's simple: You cannot teach people what you do not know. Think about preparing for a test in school; the Lord can help you as you study—to be alert, to remember the information you have studied—but if you never open a book, He will not put knowledge into your head when you haven't put forth any effort.

The Lord gave us scriptures for a reason; they contain the words He would say if He were here personally. He isn't going to give you revelation that you could have learned from the scriptures. If you've done your part in preparing, the Spirit will bring to your remembrance that which will help those you teach understand the gospel. "You are responsible to thoroughly understand the lessons and teach by the Spirit in your own words" (*Preach My Gospel,* 19).

When studying the scriptures, focus on strengthening your testimony of the Book of Mormon. It is key in strengthening your testimony of the restored gospel. Also, become more familiar with the Bible and its teachings;

depending on where you serve, many people may be familiar with the Bible. When teaching others, it helps to build on common, basic beliefs. Also study *Preach My Gospel*. It outlines the basic principles of the gospel and provides inspired guidelines on how to teach them.

Never think that you've learned everything you need to know to serve a mission. If there comes a point when you believe you know it all, you will have fallen to the bottom rung of mission preparation and will need to begin again. If you aren't humble before your mission, odds are you will be humbled during the first few weeks in the field.

The Lord once told Joseph Smith that "if a person gains more knowledge . . . in this life through his diligence . . . he will have so much the advantage in the world to come" (D&C 130:19). This also applies to preparing to teach the gospel; the knowledge you acquire before your mission will help you during your mission. The MTC is not the place to gain a testimony; it's the time to strengthen it.

And don't get caught in the trap of thinking there's just no time to build your testimony. While it's important to set a regular time for study—thus making it a priority—there are creative ways to incorporate scripture study into our lives. One sister suggested listening to conference talks and the standard works while driving. People spend a surprising amount of time in their cars, and this is a great way to study. Others have the scriptures on their tablets and phones so that whenever they have a few extra minutes, they can study. The institute study guides can be purchased through the Church distribution website. These can be helpful in providing insight and helping you to understand the historical background of the scriptures.

Physical Preparation

Health

Before serving a mission, you need to determine if you are physically and emotionally capable. When people say that it's the toughest time of their life, they are not exaggerating. It is emotionally and physically taxing. A mission can expose weaknesses in even the most fit of missionaries. Remember, emotional and physical problems are not solved on a mission; they are exacerbated.

Elder Ballard said, "Young women with serious mental, emotional, or physical limitations are excused from full-time missionary service. They shouldn't feel guilty about that. They are just as precious and important to the Church as if they were able to go into the mission field."[16] Elder Ballard further elaborated on what a missionary can do to prepare for the rigors of the mission field:

> Missionaries need to be self-reliant . . . and not be so dependent on their mother or father.
>
> They need to be able to handle the physical demands of missionary work. Young people should keep their weight under control and be physically fit. . . .
>
> Prospective missionaries need to learn to work. They ought to have a job and save money for their missions. . . . Working and saving for a mission . . . gives a young man or a young woman a good work ethic. Whatever else missionary work is, it is work!

---

16. M. Russell Ballard, "How to Prepare to Be a Good Missionary," *Liahona,* Mar. 2007, 10–15.

One mission president said that he could usually handle the sins and transgressions of a missionary, but it was their unwillingness to work that caused them to be sent home.

Clothing

You have a testimony, and you're ready to work. Now what? Along with your call, you will be provided with a specific list of what clothing to bring, but buying the appropriate clothing can be challenging, especially if your call comes in the summer and you're headed for a mission that includes chilly weather. When Ellie asked a department store clerk where they kept their long skirts, the clerk laughed at her. This was July, and long skirts weren't in stock, not even in Utah. If you get your call early enough, say, in April, and you anticipate leaving in the summer, begin shopping as soon as possible. This is especially important when buying a dress coat. You don't know where you'll be in the winter or if you'll have easy access to a store. Even if you serve in a town with a clothing store, it can be difficult to shop if you don't have a car. And if you go foreign or serve in small towns, there is a good chance there won't be any clothing stores to go to.

Don't buy cheap shoes. If you do, don't be surprised when the soles fall apart. You'll be doing a lot of walking, even if you're fortunate enough to have a car. Missionaries have calluses in three places: on their feet from walking, on their knuckles from knocking, and on their knees from praying. Those calluses are how a missionary knows she's working.

Your skirts need to be long enough to cover your knees when you're standing as well as sitting. It's better to go a little longer so you don't constantly yank on your skirt in a meeting. You will also want longer skirts if you're going to be biking. Buy outfits that are more stylish for meeting days and outfits that are more comfortable for working days. On preparation days you are still required to wear missionary attire when out in public doing your shopping and other errands. It may take some time to find skirts that work, so it's a good idea to start shopping early.

In the summer, the sisters have the advantage over the elders; skirts can be much cooler than dark slacks. But in the winter, staying warm can be a challenge. One trick for staying warm is to buy thick tights and wear long socks underneath. No one will know that you have socks on under your tights unless they look closely. Some sisters have even used ballet leggings. The sisters in Canada wear four layers—ankle-length garments, long johns, a pair of tube socks, and tights on top of it all (just be sure you buy them a size larger). If you are going to a cold climate, pack hats and scarves along with coats and warm shoes or boots.

Do whatever you have to do to stay warm. It's amazing how fast fashion cares die when you're riding your bike home at night in the dead of winter, only to have a strong wind blow your skirt over your head. That's the number-one reason that sisters pin their skirts to their bikes. (A side note: if you fall off your bike and the skirt goes with it and not you, you'll be grateful for your garments.)

In speaking of garments, there are some lessons you shouldn't have to learn the hard way. Silky bottoms and bicycles don't mix. You'll end up with very short bottoms and a wedgie. Carinessa garments are terrific for pants, but they don't work well with a skirt (a skirt tends to stick to the Carinessa fabric). The best all-around garment is the new polyester blend. It will stay in place on your bike. Mesh garments are the coolest and work well in high-humidity areas because they dry quickly. You can survive with cotton in the heat, but cotton tends to hold moisture. And you can't take enough extra sets with you; white turns to yellow quickly in the field. Some sisters prefer thermal garments for the winter, but they are only worthwhile if you are serving someplace with long, cold winters.

It is important to pay close attention to the list of required clothing provided in the packet at the time of your mission call. Your mission home will also provide you with any specific rules for your mission. Take these guidelines seriously as you shop; you don't want to take a bunch of clothes you can't wear.

In addition to clothing, missionaries may wonder what to purchase when it comes to a bike. You won't really know if you'll need one or how long you'll need it until you're in the field. For most missionaries, it's easier to buy a bike in the field. It might even be possible to purchase one from an outgoing missionary.

There is a myth in the Church that sisters don't have to ride bikes—how I wish this were true. I told the Lord I would go on a mission as long as I didn't have to ride a bike. I ended up on a bike for half my mission after not having ridden one in over ten years. A few mission presidents consider sisters on bikes immodest or unsafe, so you may not need to be on a bike, but don't count on it.

I can't count how many times I've been asked how a girl rides a bike in a skirt. My answer is, "Very carefully." You will have to buy a girl's bike—where the crossbar is diagonal instead of horizontal, which helps to keep you modest; that, however, is not enough. As mentioned, my companions and I would pin our skirts to the crossbar to keep them from flying over our heads. Skirts that pin most easily are either stretchy or flowing at the hem. My favorite cycling skirt was one made out of a jersey material that nearly touched the ground.

If you can, talk to sisters who have served in the same area in which you will be serving. Ask them what they took and what they wish they'd taken.

A few additional tips

Music can invite the Spirit like nothing else. Plan on taking inspirational music, and not just the Mormon Tabernacle Choir. EFY CDs are a good choice, as are classical composers, and there are several musicians who are safe. But, of course, plenty are questionable, so be selective. (Whatever you buy, be familiar with your mission rules first. Some missions are more selective about what missionaries may listen to.) Stock up before you leave; you may not find the CDs you want in the field. And remember, you aren't allowed to use headphones (ignoring your companion is not a good idea).

When it comes to hair and makeup, keep in mind that you won't have a lot of time to get ready in the morning. You have to be up at six thirty and you have one hour to shower, eat breakfast, put on makeup, do your hair—everything. You might tell yourself you'll get up earlier, but you're so exhausted that every minute of sleep is precious. I'm not telling you to let yourself go; nobody wants to see that. But in planning hairstyles and makeup, take into account your limited time and think low maintenance. I carted around a stupid case of hot curlers my entire mission and probably used them twice.

You get two large suitcases and one carry-on for everything. (I recommend rolling your clothes; it frees up a lot of space.) If it doesn't fit in those, don't take it or mail it home. Some sisters end up with so much useless stuff that they have to borrow their companions' luggage to get around and hope that nobody notices. People do notice, and you don't need it.

CHAPTER 4
The Missionary Training Center

WELCOME TO MISSIONARY BOOT CAMP, where you say good-bye to privacy and free time. There are several MTCs throughout the world, including ones located in Argentina, Brazil, Chile, Colombia, the Dominican Republic, England, Guatemala, Mexico, New Zealand, Peru, the Philippines, South Africa, and Spain.[17]

Your arrival and first day

When you arrive, you'll bid farewell to your family outside the MTC. Then you'll check in at the front desk and get your name tag. Take this moment to say good-bye to your first name. From here on out, you will be known as "Sister Somebody." You'll get an orange sticker on your tag that you have to wear your first day. The missionaries call this a "dork dot" (it makes it easier to herd you). With your dot prominently displayed, you will get into the first of many lines. At the end of these lines, you'll get your clothes approved (just the ones you are wearing). Then you'll receive your schedule for the next several weeks, your money card, your books (including *Preach My Gospel*), and a tetanus shot if you haven't already had one.

17. Danielle Nye Poulter, "Inside the MTC," *New Era,* Mar. 2007, 26.

You're assigned a companion for your time at the MTC, and so ends your alone time. You will go everywhere together, twenty-four seven; if your companion leaves class to use the restroom, you go to the restroom. This, of course, is also true for the mission field. In addition to the importance of "every word" being "established" in the "mouth of two or three witnesses" (2 Corinthians 13:1), being in a companionship is a protection to both of you. It can prevent sin and help you stay on track, and it can also keep you safe from worldly dangers. The only time you can be apart is when you're in your dorm, but even then, you need to be on the same floor. I was placed in a threesome, or companionship of three. The only difficult thing about this was that we were never on time to meetings because, between the three of us, someone always needed to go to the bathroom.

You are also assigned to a district, or group of ten or twelve missionaries (elders and sisters). Your district may or may not be going to your same mission, but everyone will be learning the same language. The other missionaries in your district will have arrived the same day you did and will leave the same week you do. You will attend classes with your district, eat with your district (you don't have to, but districts usually do), go to the gym with your district (my district was killer at four-square), and attend the temple together.

Districts are organized into branches, and you will be assigned to a branch president and two counselors who are local members called to serve in this capacity. They serve as any branch presidency or bishopric would. You'll meet with them the first night for an interview. They will preside over and conduct your sacrament meetings on Sundays.

The first day is a blur of meetings, rules, and new people. Most missionaries say that your first evening at the MTC is the toughest. You probably didn't get much sleep the night before, you've just said good-bye to your loved ones for what seems like forever, and you're immersed in the unknown. You sit there in that last meeting of the day thinking, *What have I done? What have I gotten myself into?* There is no going back. The only words I remember about that day were spoken by our branch president's wife. She said, "Don't worry. I guarantee you'll get more sleep tonight than you did last night." She was right.

The one thing you're given the first day that you'll depend on most is your schedule. Every minute at the MTC is scheduled out for you, from the moment you wake up at 6:30 a.m. to when you go to sleep at 10:30 p.m. You are given a half hour to get ready in the morning, which is why many sisters wake up before 6:30 a.m. You'll have one hour of total study time—half for individual study, half for companion study. Several hours of the day are spent in classes learning the doctrine you will be teaching and how to teach that doctrine. For foreign language missionaries, you will spend several hours in language study. It isn't unusual to spend four hours in a single class. Missionaries are scheduled an hour of gym time each day. There are breaks for meals and for devotionals, where you meet with several hundred missionaries. Your preparation day consists of half a day with enough time for laundry and letter writing. You are also assigned a half day to attend the temple.

The MTC is similar to a college campus. There are dorms, cafeterias, a laundry, a gym, a bookstore, and even a small medical center. Each dorm room has two bunk beds—one for you and your companion and one for another companionship. There is one large bathroom on each floor, and don't worry—the showers have curtains. Each dorm building has several floors and is exclusively for sisters or elders. You will be given a money card with a weekly allowance to use for odds and ends at the bookstore, which has a variety of items such as books, toiletries, letter-writing supplies, backpacks, CDs, and snacks (Sorry, no Mountain Dew. You'll have to find other ways to stay awake in class).

Teaching

Your teachers are returned missionaries who work at the MTC a few days a week. Usually about college age, many are men, but there are a few women. As already mentioned, most of your classes will be about learning the gospel so that you can properly teach it. Besides your scriptures, the book you will use most is *Preach My Gospel*.

It's a fact that one of the best ways to learn something is to teach it. During your classes, you will be teaching your fellow missionaries. You'll be paired off with different missionaries to practice. It's a good opportunity to learn how to adapt the lessons to meet the needs of the individual you're teaching. You'll also get to practice teaching lessons to strangers. Volunteers are invited to come to the MTC to be practiced on. You'll be assigned a time to go to a floor designed to look like an apartment building. There, you'll get to knock on a door, be invited into what looks like someone's living room, and practice what you've learned. The sessions are even videotaped so you can see how you communicate and so you can refine your skills as needed.

The call center

Most missionaries will have the opportunity to work with the phones in the Church media center. One of buildings at the MTC is like a big, religious telemarketing center. Maybe you've seen the ads on TV where the Church offers free DVDs and books. When people call to order these materials, they talk to missionaries at the MTC. This is a great opportunity to get more practice for the mission field. In addition to sending the caller any items they've requested, you will ask them if they would like representatives of the Church to visit them. (Please don't talk callers into having the missionaries come if they really don't want them. Some missionaries push people who only want the product into accepting missionaries. Most of the media contacts we received were people who avoided us and canceled appointments. They just wanted their DVDs or books dropped off without having to meet us, but we weren't allowed to do this without trying to meet them. We once drove a hundred miles [and you're only allowed so many miles per month] to deliver a copy of the Bible to a man with severe paranoia and anxiety issues. He became angry at us, and we left quickly.)

While working in the call center, you may also have the chance to field questions people have about the Church. This is a great way to get your feet wet—it isn't as scary as knocking on some random person's door.

Medical issues

While I was at the MTC, it was common for many of the sisters to suffer from headaches at first. These headaches most often resulted from a culmination of stress, exhaustion, and sitting in classes for a long time.

For most sisters, these headaches faded after the first few days. It also seemed like most missionaries caught a cold during this time as well, probably because of the close quarters. There were a few days in class when everyone in our district kept tossing around the toilet-paper roll since we were all sick.

The night before we left the MTC, a doctor spoke to all the sisters about medical issues we might face while in the field. One of the things he advised us about was that, due to the stress of a mission and being plunged into a new environment, we might not menstruate for a few months. He advised us that this was normal and said, "Sisters, I have never had a period, but if I didn't have a period for a few months, I would consider it a blessing for serving a mission." Amen to that.

The bookstore at the MTC offers medicine and feminine hygiene products, so don't worry about stocking up. Also, there is a medical center with doctors if you do require it.

CHAPTER 5
The Field

Surviving the first few weeks

MISSIONARIES SPEND A LOT OF time at the MTC wishing it was time for them to leave and trying hard not to "go over the wall" (there is a literal wall around the Provo MTC). When they finally arrive in the field, they spend the next few months wishing they were back at the MTC.

Those who have gone on a mission say it's the hardest time of their life. Don't think they're exaggerating. There are no vacations, no breaks, and no days off. Preparation days are just that—preparation. It's a good week if, on that day, you can squeeze in a basketball game or a nap. Remember, Elder Ballard said that missionary work is work. And it can be challenging.

During the first days in the field, a new missionary has all the faith of a child. She knows that every person who lets her in will be baptized, that every copy of the Book of Mormon she hands out will result in a burning testimony, and that all refusals are just seeds planted for later.

It's no wonder that many missionaries are let in on their first door approach. Only the Lord knows whether this is because of that strong faith and/or because He knows that a new missionary needs a boost of encouragement. Whatever the case, it's important to nurture that innocent faith.

At my first door approach, I asked a lady if she would like to learn more, and she said yes. My response was "Really?" During one sister's first day knocking, she said, "The next door had better let us in and offer us something to drink." Not surprisingly, at the next door, she and her companion were offered something to drink.

Before long, however, the reality of the work sets in and is a bit of a shock. You can't believe that someone can listen to your testimony or read the Book of Mormon and deny it. You are shocked when people are mean to you. You think of the loving family you left behind and wonder why you are putting yourself through this—not to mention *paying* for the privilege.

One new elder experienced that loss of innocence quicker than most. In his first district meeting, he reported how the work was going. He spoke about how awesome the work was, how awesome the ward and area were, and how they were going to baptize many. He told about one woman they had taught that week and how he was sure she would be baptized. Even when his companion reminded him that the woman had given them the wrong phone number, the elder just knew she would be baptized. The next week, that same elder reported to his district. This time he said, "I hate this area. This ward won't help us. There's no work here." The rest of the district spent the meeting "talking him off the ledge" by telling him to toughen up.

Soon-to-be missionaries hear stories about missionaries who have umpteen doors slammed in their face only to find a golden contact behind the last door. Does this happen? Yes, but rarely. What you don't hear about is how that street was part of a block, a neighborhood, a city of slammed doors. Nor do you hear about how that long day was the end of a long month of no investigators. You don't hear about how when they return to teach their golden contact, he refuses to answer his door and he's left the Book of Mormon on his porch with a note that says, "No thanks. Don't come back." This is when "endure to the end" becomes more than just words.

Many sisters enter the field unprepared for how difficult it will be. You would be surprised how many missionaries, even if they don't act on it, seriously consider returning home their first few months out. If you struggle with these thoughts, please don't think you are alone. I was miserable my first few weeks in the field. I remember telling myself that in six weeks, there would be a transfer and I could hope for a change. To survive the first six weeks—that was my goal. By the end of that time, I had settled into missionary life and was happy where I was. Don't act on your initial fears. Give it a few months then see how you feel. It takes time to adjust. You may hate life when you get there, but that doesn't mean you've made the wrong decision or that you have a weak testimony.

One sister only stayed on her mission because when she called her parents to tell them she wanted to come home, her dad said, "We're not quitters in this family." She stayed and went on to have the highest number of baptisms in her zone. Instead of letters filled with discouragement, her letters soon told about how much she loved her mission and how she couldn't imagine going home.

President Eyring teaches that being called of God, means you will experience opposition. He said, "Just as God called you and will guide you, He will magnify you. You will need that magnification. Your calling will surely bring opposition. You are in the Master's service. You are His representative. Eternal lives depend on you. He faced opposition, and He said that facing opposition would be the lot of those He called. The forces arrayed against you will try not only to frustrate your work but to bring you down."[18]

Some missions seem to be filled with more opposition than others. While some missionaries baptize dozens a month, others will be excited to go home with just one baptism. Whatever the fruits of your labors, what is most important is that a missionary serves with all her heart.

Enos speaks of his missionary work among the Lamanites. "And I bear record that the people of Nephi did seek diligently to restore the Lamanites unto the true faith in God. But our labors were vain; their hatred was fixed" (Enos 1:20). I can't tell you how many times Enos's words became mine. When Enos attempted his missionary work, it was about 500 B.C. There wasn't much success until 90 B.C., when Ammon and his brethren served their missions. It took four hundred years for the Lamanites to become ready for the gospel!

These facts can help you understand what makes a mission difficult and how you should measure your success. As a missionary, Enos was just as successful as Ammon. You may have a mission like Ammon's or Enos's. The important thing is that, like these men, you labor with all your might.

In the Book of Mormon, Jacob sees the passage of time in the parable of the olive tree. During the last harvest, or dispensation, he tells us, "The servants did go and labor with their mights; and the Lord of the vineyard labored

18. Henry B. Eyring, "Rise to Your Call," *Liahona,* Nov. 2002, 76.

also with them" (Jacob 5:72). Take comfort in the Lord's promise in Doctrine and Covenants 84:88: He will "be on your right hand and on your left, and [His] Spirit shall be in your hearts, and [His] angels round about you, to bear you up." No matter the numbers, remember whom you labor with.

Be assured that the toughest eighteen months of your life can become the most fulfilling. Each day, your life has purpose and reason. If you have the chance to reach someone, you get to see that person's life change for the better.

The first week one set of missionaries watched an investigator attend church, they doubted if she would be back for a second. She wore a low-cut, sleeveless dress that did little to hide her many tattoos. But it wasn't the tattoos or her smoker's voice that set her apart from the others; it was the hardness of her face. She wore forty years like they were seventy. She never smiled; the burdens she'd carried made that too difficult. But it wasn't a month later that she walked through those chapel doors again. Her hair had been cut to fall softly around her face, and she was wearing a long, floral-patterned dress. Once again, her face set her apart, but this time it had softened to include a smile of peace. You could physically see the result of yoking her life with Christ's.

Some have questioned the importance of a mission or the timeliness of one. "What's the rush?" they might ask. Dedicated missionaries soon realize that there are people waiting, carrying burdens almost too heavy to bear, and that, as representatives of the Savior, missionaries have the power to help alleviate those burdens in teaching them about the power of the Atonement. The Lord reminds us in Doctrine and Covenants 18:10–16,

Remember the worth of soul is great in the sight of God;

For, behold, the Lord your Redeemer suffered death in the flesh; wherefore he suffered the pain of all men, that all men might repent and come unto him.

And he hath risen again from the dead, that he might bring all men unto him, on conditions of repentance.

And how great is his joy in the soul that repenteth!

Wherefore, you are called to cry repentance unto this people.

And if it so be that you should labor all your days in crying repentance unto this people, and bring, save it be one soul unto me, how great shall be your joy with him in the kingdom of my Father!

And now, if your joy will be great with one soul that you have brought unto me into the kingdom of my Father, how great will be your joy if you should bring many souls unto me!

Successful missionaries know that it's about the one.

The schedule

A typical day begins at 6:30 a.m., followed by exercise and one hour for preparing and for breakfast. To save time, either my companion or I would shower at night so that we weren't fighting over it in the morning. If you need extra time, you can also get up earlier. You'll study the gospel for two hours in the morning, one hour on your own and one hour with your companion. At least a half hour of your personal study time must be devoted to the Book of Mormon. At 10:00, it's time to grab your coat, bag, and shoes, and you're out the door. If you're studying a foreign language, you will devote some time to that and start out a little later.

You'll spend the next few hours working. This time might be spent keeping appointments, contacting people, knocking doors, or doing service. Around noon, you take a one-hour lunch break, and then it's back to work until around 5:00, when you take an hour for dinner. Some missions are flexible about when you take meals, but some are specific. After dinner, it's back out to work until 9:30, your curfew. At night, you'll plan your next day, call and confirm your appointments, and report to your district leader if you need to. At 10:30, it's bedtime, hallelujah.

Each area has what's called an area book. In this book, you keep track of what you've taught investigators, who you're teaching, contact information, and any other pertinent facts. It's vital that you keep this up to date and readable. The first area I was in had been closed for several months, and our only clue to who had been taught was this book.

Most missions encourage time for service. Some may encourage each companionship to do four hours a week while others may not set an exact requirement. Some missionaries serve at the Goodwill, at libraries, museums, rest homes, hospitals, etc. This service can be scheduled, or missionaries can look for opportunities to help people each week.

The only days that vary from the standard schedule are Sundays and P-days (preparation days). On Sunday, you attend church, but other than that, you keep to the same schedule. On P-days, you stick with your schedule for studying, but between 9:30 and 5:00, the day is yours for laundry, shopping, naps, sports, etc. Other than general conferences and zone conferences, this will be your life for eighteen months.

You will also attend weekly meetings with your district (approximately six to eight missionaries). There, you will report on how your area is doing and be interviewed by your district leader.

Zone conference is for all missionaries within a zone. During this all-day meeting, the mission president and his assistants provide overall training, spiritual education, and safety instruction (where, for instance, you learn why you should always have your companion "back you up" when in a car. If you have a car, you or your companion has to get out and back you out every time you go in reverse. This protects you, the Church, and anyone else on the road from potential disaster. You'll quickly learn to always pull through a parking space). Most missionaries eagerly anticipate conferences. At one time in our mission, we had general conference on the weekend, P-day on Monday, and a zone conference on Tuesday. We referred to this as our "spring break" and looked forward to it for weeks prior.

There may be some variation in the schedules of different missions, but for the most part, this is what you can expect from missionary life. Even with all the routines and schedules, however, it's surprising how much freedom you're given in the field. No one is there to check up on you, get you up in the mornings, or follow you as you work. You could spend all day doing nothing, and no one besides your companion would know.

President Packer observed,

> You know, as I was presiding over the New England Mission, we had two missionaries who were 2,000 miles away from mission headquarters. And I thought one day, "That's an interesting process. You take a common, garden-variety, teenage young man; you call him on a mission; you set him apart; you give him another teenager as a companion; and you send him out someplace with a certain amount of money a month provided by himself. You then give him a simple list of instructions: no dating, rigid mission rules—spend all your time preaching and proselyting—and so on." Ofttimes, too, he's provided with an automobile. Well, it's insane when you think about it. It couldn't possibly work. The only justification is that it does.
>
> The two missionaries, 2,000 miles away, could be depended upon because somehow they had come to know that it's their church too, and He's their Lord, and this process of sustaining—the process, the simple process, of revelation relating to the call—is an operative principle of life in this church.[19]

---

19. Boyd K. Packer, "Called of God by Prophecy," *New Era*, Sep. 1978, 33.

Putting your shoulder to the wheel

During President Hinckley's first few months on his mission, he wrote his father and told him he wanted to come home. He felt he was wasting his time and his father's money. His father replied with just six words: "Forget yourself and go to work."[20]

When I look back on my mission, the times I remember as my most successful and happiest were the times I worked the hardest and longest, although much of that time showed little in the way of numbers or baptisms.

You cannot be a successful missionary if you spend time ruminating on what you're missing back home. If you're too focused on what you're missing out on, you'll miss out on your mission. As with the MTC, when you arrive in the field, all thoughts of your "former" life will not immediately leave you. Don't feel guilty for missing home; it's natural. Just don't be plagued with thoughts of what you would or could be doing if you weren't on a mission. As you work a little bit harder and study a bit longer, these thoughts will fade away.

Finding, teaching, and baptizing

A missionary can spend a good chunk of her time focusing on finding investigators.

While I saw few baptisms, I did see a few miracles. Remember the golden contact at the end of a street of slammed doors? We found that person once. We had been knocking in our area for months, and I recall only teaching one or two discussions all that time. I woke up one morning knowing the very street we needed to head

20. "Sweet Is the Work: Gordon B. Hinckley, 15th President of the Church," *New Era*, May 1995, 8.

for. I had been there long enough that I was intimately familiar with our area. We had a district meeting that morning, so it wasn't until after lunch that we made our way to that street. It made no sense to knock in that particular neighborhood; it was on the other side of our area, and we had appointments scheduled later on our side, but the impression to tract that street was surprisingly strong. It was as if the Lord was pushing us.

We biked over, knocked on a few doors, and at the right one, I explained who we were and how the Book of Mormon was another testament of Jesus Christ. The woman who answered said, "Come in and tell me more of this book." We left her a copy. Later on, we tried to teach her again, but she wasn't ready, and about a month later, our area was closed. I can't help but think that maybe, just maybe, we planted a seed.

When I entered the MTC, it was required that we memorize six discussions. I remember teaching my first discussion in the field, trying desperately to get every word right. It wasn't long until I quit trying to teach the discussion and instead tried to teach the people. Not long afterward, the First Presidency changed the discussion format to be more flexible. I think they realized that too many missionaries were using the discussions as a crutch instead of as a tool. When you don't know what you're doing, it's easy to "bluff," or repeat someone else's words. Remember, the lessons are the knowledge, but you are the teacher. You must decide how to use that knowledge in the best interests of your investigators, as directed by the Spirit.

If you're privileged enough to have someone willing to share a few moments of their time with you, don't waste it telling them what you think they ought to hear; tell them what the Lord thinks they ought to hear. Above all, listen to the Spirit; it'll usually tell you what you need to say. I remember stopping a first discussion to begin reading a chapter out of the Book of Mormon with a young woman. We hadn't even introduced the book to her or even mentioned Joseph Smith, but I felt she needed to hear Alma 36; she needed to hear the joy Alma the Younger felt at his repentance. She began reading the Book of Mormon after that.

Miracles happen when missionaries listen to the Spirit. Before the change in curriculum, two sisters were working with a young woman who had been inactive for a long time. They were teaching her the second discussion, which lists the first principles of the gospel. When they reached the section on baptism, the senior companion stopped, sensing that since the woman they were teaching had already been baptized, she didn't need to hear this. They instead began teaching her about the sacrament and its purpose, explaining that since members can't be baptized over again when they sin, the Lord instituted the sacrament so that they can renew their baptismal covenants each week and gain forgiveness. The missionaries taught her that the principles of the gospel that lead nonmembers to the baptismal font—faith and repentance—are the same principles that lead members to the sacrament table.

They were surprised when the woman began to cry. She told them it was difficult for her to attend church because she wasn't allowed to partake of the sacrament since she had been disfellowshipped. Had they known, they probably wouldn't have dared broach such a painful subject. Thank goodness they hadn't known, because in that moment, because they had listened to the Spirit and focused on her needs, they and the woman were given the opportunity to understand with complete clarity the purpose of the sacrament and of being disfellowshipped.

The missionaries wept the day they were told that she had received her endowment and was married in the temple. All that memorization at the MTC had placed the knowledge in their minds, but it wasn't until they taught by the Spirit that they understood it.

One of the most important skills a missionary needs to acquire on her mission is the ability to listen to those she is teaching. Often, missionaries jump in to answer a question they've just asked an investigator. Don't be afraid of silence. You may be asking investigators deep, spiritual questions about subjects they may have never even considered. Give them a moment to think about what you have asked them.

If you ask someone who hasn't known God what they think God is like, it may take them a few moments to come up with an answer. A gospel principle is much more powerful when the learning is internalized by the student than if it merely comes from the teacher. When a long silence becomes awkward, however, it's okay for you to help them. Once you've acquired the ability to listen, you'll know better when it's time to talk.

You cannot progress in your teaching if your investigator has a concern you ignore. As a new missionary, I would often pass over concerns my investigators had because their questions pertained to material in another discussion. Imagine teaching someone who's afraid that there is no life after death, and you go on about the Restoration of the Church, thinking the entire time, *I can't wait until later when we get to teach him the plan of salvation.* Remember, we teach the investigator, not the lesson.

I stood at the door of one home and listened as one sister argued with the woman inside. The woman kept saying there could be no more word from God, while the missionary kept saying how the woman should read the Book of Mormon because it was more word from God. What was the woman's concern? She didn't believe in more scripture, and there we were, forcing more scripture on her. But until the woman had resolved that concern, she wouldn't accept any book from us. We might have been better off to address her beliefs in a respectful manner and explain why we believed differently and bear testimony. I doubt the outcome would have been different that day, but perhaps we could have left her with something to ponder instead of with anger. I have a sad feeling that the next time she sees two missionaries at her door, she won't open it because all she'll remember from those Mormons is contention.

Prayer and fasting

When your will is in line with the Father's, you will see success. As mentioned earlier, the Bible Dictionary defines prayer as bringing the will of the child in sync with the will of the Father. When you are a missionary and dedicating yourself to Him, it seems the Lord answers your prayers more readily than at other times in your life, which is not surprising. The channel of communication between you and the Lord is much more clear on a mission since you've drowned out the interference of the world.

There were two elders who'd been knocking all day without success. One elder said a prayer in his heart that they would be invited in at the next house. Sure enough, the lady at the very next house let them in. Of course, it was a little old lady who offered to let them see her antique Bible and then immediately ordered them back out, but they were grateful because the Lord answered their specific prayer, nonetheless.

Which takes us to our next lesson. Remember Joseph Smith and the lost 116 manuscript pages? Be careful what you pray for—you just might get it. Two sisters had been knocking all day and were walking a couple of miles to their dinner appointment when they passed an Italian restaurant. The smell was enticing, and they thought about how nice it would be to go out to dinner for a change. When they arrived at their dinner appointment, they were told that the members' oven had broken. The wife had just discovered it when she'd pulled a still-raw roast from the oven. They asked the sisters where they wanted to go for dinner, to which the sisters replied that anywhere was fine. The family took them to an Italian restaurant. While they enjoyed the meal a great deal, they did feel a little guilty about the timing of their wish and the broken oven.

Another set of sisters had almost the same experience, only instead of a broken oven, the member had accidentally set her glass casserole dish on a hot burner. The dish exploded, and the member turned to the sisters and asked, "Which one of y'all prayed that we'd go out to dinner?"

Not all prayers are answered as promptly these. Prayers such as *Let them be baptized before I'm transferred* depend upon someone else's agency. The Lord can't force any one into the water any more than you can. All you can do is make sure you're in the right place so that you're ready when the time is right. Remember, prayer is the act of uniting your will with the Father's, and sometimes what you're asking isn't His will.

The sons of Mosiah "had given themselves to much prayer, and fasting; therefore they had the spirit of prophecy, and the spirit of revelation, and when they taught, they taught with power and authority of God. . . . having had much success in bringing many to the knowledge of the truth" (Alma 17:3–4). But even with their successes, these missionaries knew their limitations. Of themselves, they were nothing, so they "prayed much that the Lord would grant unto them a portion of his Spirit to go with them, and abide with them, that they might be an instrument in the hands of God to bring, if it were possible, their brethren . . . to the knowledge of the truth" (Alma 17:9).

The sons of Mosiah realized that only the Lord knew the hearts of those they were teaching. They simply prayed to be instruments for the Lord, trusting in His arm rather than in the arm of flesh. What a perfect prayer to have constantly with you.

However, when praying is not enough, you can learn from the sons of Mosiah again. Notice that Alma 17:9 also says that the four missionaries fasted for success. One sister prayed with all the faith she could muster that she and her companion would have an investigator at church the next Sunday. They had been working hard for three months and had nothing to show for it. As she prayed about this, the thought came to her that to show the Lord she really wanted an investigator at church, she should fast. They had a few appointments that day with people who had invited them back, so she was hopeful they might convince at least one of them to come to church. Unfortunately, all of their appointments fell through, and they spent the next two days tracting. The only person who agreed to listen to them was a drunken elderly man who wanted to talk to some young, pretty girls.

That Sunday morning, the sister tried to remain hopeful. Exercising faith, she prepared the lesson for the Gospel Principles class, which they taught whenever they had an investigator. As church began, her hope wavered as no new faces came through the door. But a few minutes into the meeting, a less-active family they had visited awhile before walked in. The family's twenty-something son, who up until then had refused the missionary lessons, was with them. After sacrament meeting, he told them he was ready for the lessons. That week, the sister missionary taught her first Gospel Principles lesson to an investigator.

The Lord hears and answers prayers—from simple requests for food to heartfelt pleas of the faithful.

Study

On a typical day, a missionary has two hours to study the gospel. Why does the Lord give a missionary so much study time when there are people waiting to hear the gospel? He answered that question in a revelation to Joseph Smith in 1829: "Seek not to declare my word, but *first* seek to obtain my word, and *then* shall your tongue be loosed; *then,* if you desire, you shall have my Spirit and my word . . . unto the convincing of men" (D&C 11:21; emphasis added).

You cannot teach people that which you do not know, and the Spirit can't draw from an empty well. When you study, study with the intent to uplift and teach, not to argue. I learned from personal experience that the Spirit won't support you when you engage in debate. The instant I became contentious about the doctrine, all those awesome scriptures I'd studied slipped from my mind and left me a tongue-tied fool.

One of the ways the Lord speaks to His children is through the scriptures. If you're not studying the scriptures, one of the strongest and clearest conduits you have to heaven is closed. Wilford Woodruff once said that by studying the scriptures, one can "learn to comprehend the mind and will of God."[21] As a missionary, it is essential to comprehend the mind and will of God. You will find great treasures of knowledge as you search the scriptures, both ancient and modern, and the other materials the Church has provided for missionaries and members.

Preach My Gospel is an invaluable tool for learning the gospel, but more importantly, it will help you learn how to teach the gospel. "It is intended to help you be a better-prepared, more spiritually mature missionary, and a more persuasive teacher. We urge you to use it daily in your personal and companion preparation" (*Preach My Gospel*, v).

Obedience

Successful missions require complete obedience. Missionaries are often surprised to arrive in the field and realize that they and their companion are completely on their own. You and your companion could spend the entire day in bed and no one would be the wiser. Making your mission successful is completely up to you and your obedience to the rules. (This is another reason it is so important that you

21. *Contributor,* August 1895, 639.

serve for the right reasons; a missionary without motivation will find obedience oppressive.)

A lack of obedience prevents progression and precludes the reception of blessings. If you sleep in and don't study in the morning, chances are you won't have the inspiration you need to teach your investigators what the Lord wants them to hear. If you give up on tracting and go home an hour early, you may have missed your golden contact. If you slack off one day and hang out at the mall, someone may see you and decide not to give you that member referral you had been hoping for because they can't trust that you are who you profess to be.

Remember, "when we obtain any blessing from God, it is by obedience to that law upon which it is predicated" (D&C 130:21). When you are in the field, you will have as much agency to choose between good or evil as when you are at home.

Areas and companions

My first area was fifty miles from the nearest missionaries. We were dropped off and told, "Good luck." The area had been closed for several months, so we started with nothing. Not only did I know nothing about missionary work, but half the town spoke only Spanish, and I didn't. I was thankful for my experienced, Spanish-speaking companion, but I struggled to live and work with a stranger. I wasn't used to being told what do to or living with someone in such close quarters. She spoke the language fluently, and I was left feeling that nothing I did was right and that my only purpose was to be her companion. I sat there, forcing a smile, while she talked to investigators.

In our mission, transfers came every six weeks. I told myself to hang in there; I could stand anything for that amount of time. I prayed for a transfer. Four and a half months later, I was praying to stay for just one more transfer. It had taken a long time, but the work was finally progressing, and so was I. The investigators seemed to appreciate my broken attempts at Spanish, and the branch had become my new family. I cried the day I boarded the transfer van.

Areas and companions are much the same. Some you like immediately, some take more time to enjoy, and some compel you to make the best of a difficult situation. You'll have companions who become your best friend the first day and companions that make you wonder if it's a cruel joke that you've been placed with your exact opposite in everything.

If you have a companion you don't get along with, remember that everyone has their own idiosyncrasies. The key is tolerance coupled with compromise. Sister Johnson saw herself as easygoing and her companion, Sister Smith, as borderline obsessive-compulsive. Sister Smith wasn't OCD, but she did like order. It drove Sister Johnson crazy that everything had to be just so, and at times, she purposely did small things to prove that everything didn't need to be perfect. Case in point: Sister Smith insisted they put their detergent in the washing machine before the clothes; Sister Johnson just tossed it in after. If Sister Johnson put her clothes in before the soap, Sister Smith would pull everything out and put the soap in first. Sister Johnson couldn't help but wonder why it was such a big deal for her companion, and she purposely started throwing her clothes in with the detergent, just to see what happened and to prove a point. Meanwhile, Sister Smith was thinking, *Doesn't she understand that this prevents the soap from being stuck in the clothes?*

After several weeks of silent battling, Sister Johnson still wondered why it mattered at what point the detergent went in. However, this time, she had an epiphany: If it really didn't matter, but it did matter to her companion, why not let her put it in first?

This silent war sounds like a trivial thing, but companionships have been damaged with less. The key is to realize that not everyone thinks like you and you won't agree all the time or even much of the time. Use each other's strengths to your benefit, and be willing to go her way sometimes.

Some difficulties in companionships go beyond personality clashes. There are companions who refuse to work or keep mission rules. (This seems to be more of a problem among the elders, especially with those who serve for the wrong reasons.) While the majority of your companions will be okay, remember that if you're stuck with a problem companion, transfer day will come. If an inspired mission president has put you together, even though you can't see it at the time, trust that there's a purpose in all things and try to see what you can learn from it. Until then, try talking to your companion. Missionaries can get into lazy habits without even being aware of it. They may have slipped into bad habits due to sickness, exhaustion, trunkiness, or homesickness. Missionaries are to hold companion inventory once a week, where they discuss any problems they may have. This is a good time to approach your companion with an understanding, open mind. It might be enough to bring them back or, in the event of illness, encourage them to get help. (Word to the wise: Try to avoid having companionship inventory when you're both suffering from PMS.)

Most problems between companions can be solved without taking your leaders away from their work. However, if you've done everything you can and your companion is holding the work back, discuss the problem with your district leader to determine possible solutions. Don't use your weekly meeting with this elder to complain. It's more effective to express your concerns and your desires to fix the problem. If your companion is seriously breaking mission rules, you must bring this to the attention of your leaders. Don't be concerned about your companion being sent home; this rarely happens—especially if the infraction is brought up before it gets too serious. Remember, though, that most issues can be handled within the companionship.

Safety

Sisters are often naive when it comes to personal safety. While on my mission, I was hooted and hollered at, hit on (by mostly crazy people), flashed, pinched in the behind, and received the occasional drunken midnight phone call. One companion had to be transferred when a predator started stalking her. So what's a girl to do? Think smart. Even though missionaries are often blessed with a measure of heavenly protection, you will experience the consequences of agency used unwisely. Poor choices include, but are not limited to, going into a man's house without a third woman, giving your phone number to strangers, telling strangers where you live, going into unsafe areas after dark, and flirting with men.

While some of these things seem like common sense, you may be wondering how you teach people without going into their homes or without giving them contact information. In order to protect you, the Church has clear rules when it comes to teaching members of the opposite sex. You cannot teach a man alone. If you're tracting and a man invites you to come in, don't. If possible, share a quick message on the doorstep, then, if you feel he's interested, set up an appointment for later. When teaching him again, you must take another sister, probably someone from the ward or branch, with you. If there are elders nearby, you can ask them to teach him.

Not only is turning a man over to the elders safer; it's a good way to weed out the interested investigators from the players feigning interest because a pretty girl is at their door. Some men will always want to talk to a girl who shows up at their door, especially if they've been drinking. After getting hit on one too many times, we had to stop knocking on doors on weekends in some of our areas.

If a strange man wants your phone number and you don't feel comfortable giving it to him, you can always hand him a pass-along card with the phone number of the Church's media center and he can request missionaries thereby. And since no one is allowed in your apartment but authorized missionaries, there is no reason to give your address to an investigator.

CHAPTER 6
Coming Home

What now?

WELL, YOU'RE HOME. ADMIT IT—there were days, weeks, even months where you thought your mission would never end. But there were times when you prayed it wouldn't.

Wouldn't it be nice if there were a WTC (World Training Center)? A place that taught classes such as Dating 101, "Does He Like Me (and if not, how do I get him to?)," or "What Do I Wear Now?"

While I was serving my mission, low-rise pants became the norm. When I went shopping, I grabbed a pair of pants without thinking to check anything but the size. When the pants stopped a good four inches below my garment waistband and not so much above my behind, I almost cried. It took work and a bit of creativity to find clothes I could actually wear.

Unfortunately, I'm not qualified to give advice on dating or clothes (mostly because the rules and styles may have changed by the time you read this), but I can help you with other adjustments.

You'd be surprised how difficult coming home can be for some missionaries. When you leave home, you're relatively sure you will see your loved ones again. But when you leave the mission field, you may never again see those you've come to love.

"'Coming home after serving my full-time mission was harder than leaving home had been,' said a young Canadian returned missionary. 'I'm usually not an emotional person,' he added, 'but during the first months after I returned home, I felt a great deal of emotion. Often I didn't understand my mixed-up feelings. At times, I would go to bed at night and cry. I was embarrassed and put on a front for my family and friends because I didn't want them to know.'"[22]

Maintaining your spirituality

You may also find that maintaining the high level of spirituality you experienced in the mission field is more difficult at home, which is understandable. In the field, you're studying at least two hours a day, teaching the gospel, and constantly thinking about and doing spiritual things. So it's important when you come home that you keep up regular scripture study, even if it isn't for two hours a day. Stay active in the Church, accept and magnify any callings that come your way, and participate in every way you can. Remember to act on what you've been teaching for the last eighteen months.

When missionaries return home, they often become stagnant. On your mission, your time was scheduled tightly, and you knew what was expected of you. There are leaders to give direction and guidance and companions to help keep you on task. Some missionaries come home and do nothing because they are unsure what to do and don't have anyone to push them. Some

22. Bruce L. Olsen, "Home from a Mission," *Ensign,* June 1991, 46.

returned missionaries miss not having someone to make all their big decisions for them. There were no bills to worry about, they didn't have to figure out where they'd live, and they didn't have to decide what they were going to do with their life. Some returned missionaries procrastinate making any decision because they are afraid of making the wrong one.

Don't fall into this trap. Give yourself a time frame to find a job or get back into school, even if it's just a temporary situation, until you decide what you really want to do. Don't procrastinate making a decision just because you don't know what the right decision is. Much as with deciding to go on a mission, you just have to move forward in life and then you'll know what it is you're supposed to do.

CHAPTER 7
Quick, Easy, and Delicious Recipes for the Field

IN SOME MISSIONS, YOU WILL be cooking most of your meals; in others, you will be eating with members for most dinners. It all depends on mission rules. Some missions discourage missionaries from eating with families unless there is a nonmember present. But even if you eat with members often, count on fixing your own meals as well.

Since you're only allotted an hour for mealtime, it's important to be able to whip up something fast. When you do cook, try to cook more than two portions so you have meals for multiple days. To stay healthy, it's important to eat a balanced diet at your apartment since you can't control what you eat in the homes of members. Keep plenty of fruits and vegetables on hand, and always take a healthy snack—not to mention plenty of water—with you when you go out tracting.

Your apartment should come equipped with basic cooking utensils and dishes. It will, however, be up to you to stock it with food using your weekly allowance. If you are careful in your spending, this allowance will provide for your basic needs. You may even have money left over each month since there is little else you need to buy on a mission.

Since there's very little time in the morning for
cooking, you may end up eating a lot of cereal, depending
on where you serve. Although cold cereal makes for a
quick, easy meal, it provides the kind of energy that is
quickly burned. Try alternating cold cereal with breakfasts
that include protein to sustain you through long days on
your feet or bicycle. On P-day, boil several eggs for the
week. Then, for breakfast, you can simply peel an egg,
make some toast, and have an orange or banana. This
makes a healthy, fast breakfast that will fuel you for the
day. You can also boil oatmeal or Cream of Wheat in just a
few minutes.

Sandwiches and salads plus fruit make for good lunches;
just be careful what you put in them. Pile them high with
lots of veggies, and go with low-fat dressings. Don't get
sucked into diet shakes. These are chock-full of sugar and
will leave you feeling hungry.

Shepherd's Pie
1 pound ground beef
1 small onion
1 can cream of mushroom soup
1 can peas
1 package instant mashed potatoes (makes about 2 cups)
1 cup grated cheese

Brown ground beef and onion in a skillet; drain.
While frying meat, cook mashed potatoes according
to microwave directions on package, then set aside.
When meat is done, add the soup and peas, then scoop
mixture into 9x9-inch square baking pan. Spread mashed
potatoes over meat mixture. Sprinkle cheese over top.

Bake for 15 minutes at 350 degrees or until cheese is melted. Makes four servings.

Macaroni and Cheese

1 quart water
1 bag uncooked macaroni
1 pound ground beef
1 can condensed tomato soup
1 cup grated cheese

Bring water to a boil and add noodles. While water is boiling, brown ground beef in a skillet; drain. When noodles are soft, drain and add to cooked ground beef still in the skillet. Mix in tomato soup. Sprinkle cheese over top. Place skillet in warm oven until cheese melts. Serve with a small salad. Makes about 4 servings.

Institute Chocolate Chip Cookies

This recipe was used by our senior missionaries to entice students to attend the local institute. It attracted the missionaries as well.

1/2 pound unsalted butter
3/4 cup sugar
1 cup brown sugar
2 eggs
1 tablespoon vanilla
3 cups flour
3/4 teaspoon salt
3/4 teaspoon baking soda
3 cups chocolate chips

Combine all ingredients in order except chocolate chips. Blend with a mixer; stir in chocolate chips. Dough will appear dry. Roll dough into 1-inch balls, place on an ungreased cookie sheet, and bake at 350 degrees for 6–8 minutes. Cookies should be slightly brown on bottom but still appear doughy on top. Remove cookies from the sheet and place them on the counter, where they will harden slightly but stay incredibly soft.

Chicken Wads
1 can chicken
8 ounces cream cheese
Tony's Seasoning (or salt, garlic, and pepper), to taste
1 can ready-to-bake crescent rolls

Mix together chicken, cream cheese, and seasoning. Roll out each crescent-roll dough triangle. Spoon chicken mixture in each one, and wrap up in rolls. Bake at 350 degrees until light brown.

Frito Pie
1 can chili
Handful Fritos chips
Cheese

Heat chili in the microwave. Layer Fritos chips in a bowl, and pour chili over top. Sprinkle cheese on top. This makes a fast lunch.

Spaghetti
1 quart water
1/2 bag spaghetti pasta
1 pound ground beef
2 small zucchini, cut into 1-inch pieces
1 jar spaghetti sauce of your choice

In a large saucepan, bring water to boil. Break noodles in half and drop in pan. While waiting for the noodles to boil, brown ground beef in a skillet. Toss the zucchini into the ground beef when ground beef's about halfway done. It will cook in the juices. Boil pasta for about 10 minutes or until soft. (If you throw a piece of pasta at the wall and it sticks, it's done.) Mix spaghetti sauce in with ground beef. You can mix noodles in as well or serve separately. Makes about 4 servings.

Rice and Chicken
2 cups instant rice
1 pound chicken, cut into 1-inch pieces
1 can cream of chicken soup
1/2 cup reduced-fat cheese
Salt and pepper to taste

Cook rice according to package directions. While rice is cooking, brown chicken in a saucepan over medium heat until white all the way through. Combine rice, chicken, soup, and cheese in medium-sized bowl, and stir with a spoon until evenly mixed. Salt and pepper to taste. Serve with veggies. Makes about 4 servings.

Burritos

1 pound ground beef
1 can refried beans
1 cup grated cheese
4 tortillas
1 cup salsa
4 cups lettuce

Brown ground beef in a large saucepan. Drain fat. Mix in beans and cheese. Warm one tortilla in between two slightly damp paper towels in the microwave. Put a quarter of the bean mixture in one tortilla with 1 cup lettuce and 1/4 cup salsa. Makes 4 servings.

CHAPTER 8
A Brief Summary and Words of Wisdom from
Those Who've Gone Before

Do sister missionaries ride bikes?
Yes, even in stateside missions. This particular decision is up to the mission president. Some presidents won't put sisters on bikes, but some do.

How do you ride a bike in a skirt?
Two words: safety pins (large ones). You will need to purchase a girl-style bike, one where the crossbar drops down instead of going across. Wrap the front of your skirt around this bar and pin it underneath.

What happens if I fall off my bike?
Don't. And if you do, be glad you're wearing garments.

Will I actually be going door to door?
Most likely, you will be tracting at least some of the time in your mission. How much depends on the mission. In some missions, it is difficult to go door to door so missionaries do what's called street contacting, where they approach people on the street. Even sisters called to the visitors' centers will spend some time in the field. Wherever you go, be prepared to talk to strangers.

What type of clothes should I buy?

Outside of following the guidelines in your call, keep in mind any specific guidelines provided by the mission shortly after your call. Some missions are stricter with regard to colors, prints, and shoes. Also, requirements can change with the weather. You don't want to buy a bunch of clothes you can't wear and have to buy new clothes when you enter the field. For general guidelines and photographs see the Church's website: missionary.lds.org/dress-grooming/sister. And take plenty of garments.

Will I gain weight on my mission?

Possibly, but not necessarily. Whether or not you gain a significant amount weight on your mission is up to you. Aside from dinner appointments, you control what and how much you eat. There is also a half hour of exercise time built into your daily schedule, not to mention all of the walking and biking you may be doing. You may see some weight fluctuations due to changes in lifestyle and the stress you undergo. Some sisters actually didn't gain weight until they came home because the amount of physical activity they were used to dropped so drastically.

Often sisters are worried about eating too much when they're invited to dinner because they don't want to insult the family by not eating a lot. The key is to eat slowly so it looks like you're eating a lot.

How do I keep my feet from smelling and scaring off investigators and companions?

Smelly feet are the bane of all nylon-wearing sister missionaries. I know—gross. To keep the smell at bay, buy some foot powder and pour a little in your shoes before going out each morning.

Do you really call your companion "sister"?

It may sound strange to always call someone you live with "sister," but it feels perfectly normal. What will be strange is when you both return home and try calling each other by your first names.

Do sisters have more success than elders?

Not necessarily. Sisters are able to get in more doors when tracting because, let's face it, it's less intimidating to let women into your house than men. However, when it comes to actual teaching, it's the quality of the missionary, not the gender.

How many sisters are in the field versus elders?

It depends on where you serve. Some missions with visitors' centers will have higher numbers of sister. And with the change in age, more sisters are going.

Will I get along with my companion?

There are companions you will love, companions you will like, and companions you will barely tolerate. You might be assigned to a companion with whom you have nothing in common, and you might end up with one who refuses to work. As long as your companion is willing to work, you'll usually be able to smooth out any differences. Remember, try to focus on each other's strengths. You may never be best friends, but any unity you can achieve will allow you to focus on the work instead of the companionship.

It can be more difficult to deal with a companion who refuses to work. If it goes on longer than a few days and you've spoken to her about it, feel free to talk to your district leader. Remember to try to work things out with your companion before you take it to your leaders. And, if all else fails, remind yourself that this too shall pass—transfers are coming.

GLOSSARY OF MISSION TERMS

Assistant to the president (AP): Two elders called by the mission president as his assistants. These guys travel the mission checking on and training the other missionaries. I've heard rumors of sister assistants who work with the mission president's wife and provide training to the sisters, but I've never had this confirmed.

District: All missions are organized into groups and subgroups, just as the Church is. A district would be equivalent to a ward or branch.

Exchanges (splits): When a companionship divides up and each sister goes with another missionary or a ward member for a short period of time.

Greenies: Refers to missionaries from the time they enter the field until their first transfer (six weeks in the field). When other new missionaries come in, the six-weekers are no longer referred to as greenies.

Golden question (GQ): The GQ consists of two parts. After you introduce yourself and the Church to someone, you ask if they'd like to learn more.

Golden contact: An investigator who is ready for the gospel and prepared to make commitments.

Media contact: A person who calls the Church after seeing one of our ads or visiting the Church website and who requests representatives to come visit them.

Splits: See *Exchanges.*

Trainers: When missionaries arrive in the field, they are assigned to an experienced missionary who will train them.

Transfers: Every six weeks (the time can vary in some missions), missionaries can be reassigned to a new area and companion. You may not necessarily change each transfer, but you could. Most missionaries stay in one area for at least two transfers. Transfer calls usually come right before preparation day to give you a day to pack up and say good-bye.

Trunkiness: Experiencing homesickness to the extent that it affects the work. This happens more toward the end of your mission.

Zone: All missions are organized into groups and subgroups, just as the Church is. A zone would be equivalent to a stake.

Zone conference: Once per transfer, you meet with the missionaries in your zone and receive instruction from the mission president and APs.